Six-Word Lessons for

SUCCESSFUL
START-UPS

100 Lessons to Guide
Your Company
to Success

Maureen Daniek

Published by Pacelli Publishing
Bellevue, Washington

SIX
~WORD
LESSONS

Six-Word Lessons for Successful Start-ups

Copyright © 2012, 2017 by Maureen Daniek

Published by Pacelli Publishing
9905 Lake Washington Blvd. NE, #D-103
Bellevue, Washington 98004
Pacellipublishing.com

Cover and interior design by Pacelli Publishing
Cover image by Pixabay

ISBN-10: 1-933750-31-6
ISBN-13: 978-1-933750-31-6

L egend has it that Ernest Hemingway was challenged by some friends to write a story in six words. He responded to the challenge with the following story: *For sale: baby shoes, never worn.*

Lonnie Pacelli, the series creator, believes this style of writing applies to today's culture of text messages, tweets and wall posts. Thus the inspiration for **Six-Word Lessons**.

This format seemed perfect for sharing the wide variety of lessons I have learned starting businesses—certainly even more than the 100 in this book. A lengthy chapter could easily be written on each of these lessons. I have distilled the "nuggets" for those of you who are not inclined to read lengthy books. Consider these as "appetizers" if you are considering a start-up business of your own. I hope this book will give you food for thought, ideas to think about and explore more deeply.

I am writing about my own personal experiences in several start-up businesses. These lessons came from start-ups that began with a group of people and then grew quickly. If you own a small business by yourself and bootstrap with your own funds, some of these lessons may not apply to you. Many of my experiences were enlightening and rewarding and others were challenging. Upon reflection the best way I have found to integrate these experiences has been with a judicious use of humor.

I hope you learn from and use some of the ideas in this book, and I wish you success in your business venture.

Let me know how it has impacted you at Maureen@maureendaniek.com.

Table of Contents

The Raw Excitement of New Beginnings

1

Do you have blood type E?

Is entrepreneurship in your blood? Is your mind bubbling with ideas and "why not" phrases? Are you a risk taker? Do you love to seize new ideas and take action? Does the lack of resources juice your creativity? If yes, you just might be an entrepreneur.

The giddiness of a new idea.

There's nothing like the high of creating a new innovation, and the possibility of building the next big thing. Being part of a team united in a vision that can possibly make a revolutionary impact is an enthralling experience!

3

Protecting and feeding your budding dream

Hold your business baby close in the infancy. It is precious and fragile. Well meaning or jealous friends and family will try to shoot it down "for your protection." You need non-risk adverse buddies right now.

Draw people you know and trust.

In the chaotic early days you need to know that your partners have your back. It helps to start with proven relationships that have weathered and survived storms. You want to already know how your partners will look when things get ugly.

5

Underdog beginnings draw the passionate ones.

Before the money comes, people are drawn by the challenge, the thrill of something groundbreaking, and the feeling of, "us against the world." There is a connection, sense of community, and bonding like no other time that follows.

Getting started with people day one

When you start without money you have to think carefully about giving away ownership in the company. Are you exchanging equity for sweat? Will the shares vest over time, and if so, how much time? Get legal advice early on.

7

Don't leave family in the dust.

It is easy to get swallowed up in the narcotic of a start-up and put family on the back burner. Beware. You need that family support in the rough early years when things start to tumble and money is stretched tight.

Business plans are living breathing documents.

Everyone will tell you that you need to re-do your business plan. Soon you will be doing nothing but. Business plans are important but they will be out of date by tomorrow. Create them based on the purpose--for you or investors?

9

The proof is in the pudding.

Don't forget to do your beta testing. You need to show a proof of concept for a new idea or new invention. Does it work? Have you stirred out all the lumps? It is easier to fix problems earlier than later.

Who wants your shiny new toy?

Set up your focus groups and do your research early. Just because you love it doesn't mean enough other somebodies will want or need it. Is it appealing to your audience? Will your target market pay for it?

11

Create an attention-grabbing elevator pitch.

Don't underestimate how challenging this is. To get your product or concept launched you need a sound bite with a hook. Your pitch needs to be clear, concise and clever, and it must roll off your silver tongue with ease.

12

Marketing: love it or hate it.

You are nobody until you are known. You will spend a disgusting amount of money on marketing, and it will take you hostage, but you can't go anywhere without it, so better make friends with it-- fast!

13

A clever brand maven is gold.

Yes, it is all about perception and image and superficial things like that. Someone on your team needs to be able to tap into the psyche of your target market and bullseye their deepest longing. Think Mercedes, Prada, Nike, Coke, and Apple.

14

Who wants to think about exit?

It is hard to think and talk about death when you feel like you are just getting born, however time goes fast and your desired exit will determine a lot of decisions along the way. Start planning for a triumphant wake!

That Thing we Hate Talking About

15

Waiting tables to get you by

Get reacquainted with Top Ramen, brush up on your service skills, or parlay a special talent into a part-time contracting job. The first one to two years are rough financially and rarely break a profit. Think of this as building muscle.

16

Bare bones bootstrapping--lean and mean

What do you really need? Be honest. Paring down to the essentials will help you get laser focused—a table, computer, internet access, materials for products, basic collateral, and access to your target market. This is no time for fluff or fancy new computers.

17

Recall the strategies of your ancestors.

Trade beads, barter chickens for labor, help folks with their remodel, and charm your friends into helping out. Use cash to purchase only as a last resort. You will be amazed at what you can pull off without the green stuff.

18

These will be the best days.

You will look back on these early days of living on the edge and laugh about the silly and courageous and surprising events that occurred. There was tension and chaos, bonding and laughter, and the discovery of strength you never knew you had.

19

Pound of flesh in the game

How much skin are you willing to put in? Blood, sweat and tears are one thing, but there comes a time when your life feels squeezed. How much are you willing to wager on yourself? How much do you believe in the team? How much will you sacrifice?

How much money to get liftoff?

As you move forward there comes a time when cash is king. You need the green stuff to get launched. This is where wisdom, gut, and instincts come into play. How much, from what source, and how many fingers will it cost you?

21

Who is minding the cash box?

Find a trusted penny pincher to keep tight financial controls on expenses-- before the budget gets bloated. You ideal controller doesn't care about being liked or loved. They will protect the funds like their very own.

22

Begin courting potential investors early on.

Ideally you won't need them but just in case, start building relationships early on for connections, resources, and just maybe investment. Don't give up majority ownership unless this is a planned quick flip and you are on your way to Tahiti.

23

Money changes everything, my, oh my!

I thought we were friends, what happened? Now we are quibbling about salaries, shares, titles, and who has the best view. Who deserves more? The primitive reptilian brain emerges and competition threatens relationships.

24

Whoever owns the chips will rule.

When investors come, they will want seats on the board and a say in major decisions. They may even want your seat. How much of a bind are you in, and how desperate are you? How much will you give up? Pay careful attention.

25

Scent of success brings vultures swooping

Even long lost relatives will come knocking when word is out of your up-and-coming success. Investors, consultants, and other companies will descend upon you when the smell of money and success leaks out the door. Beware of the cockroaches!

The smallest investors demand the most.

You will be surprised and cornered time and again by the tedious questions from the tiniest investors who are putting money into a start-up for the first time. They want information and promises and reassurances you have little capacity to give.

27

Professional investors are not your friends.

Venture capitalists are in business to make money and make money fast. They aren't there to make your dreams come true or save your tush. Like owners of sports teams, they won't hesitate to trade out teams if need be.

28

Investment comes in and culture changes.

Put on your armor. Decisions are made based on the bottom line. Decision makers change. Employees see the big money and want a bigger piece of pie. You will think you woke up in a different company—and you did.

Risk, Failure, and Trial by Fire

29

The game of business is RISK.

Every step you take, every decision you make involves some degree of risk. Can you handle the worst case scenario? Can you mitigate the potential risks? You are often on a high-wire balancing act--get good toe shoes and stay sober.

Roller coasters and whiplashes are normal.

Anything and everything can happen and it will. Be ready to flex and change course on a dime. At the last minute, a client refuses to sign the contract. Your key employee leaves abruptly. You are left whirling in the dust.

31

If you thrive on a challenge

The challenges will be like an IV transfusion of your drug of choice. Markets change, the economy shifts, affiliate companies get cold feet, investors get nervous, you lose your rental space, you get behind in employee wages, and suddenly you've gone off your own fiscal cliff.

32

Who holds the "secret sauce" recipe?

Someone holds the intellectual property (IP)—the secret to making everything work, the ingredient that makes your company unique. That better be you or someone who'd die for you! You don't want someone walking off with it.

33

What does your success depend upon?

What factors in the economy, culture, or political system is your success linked to? Educate yourself about all the relevant issues that you need to track. Also, know the culture, environment, and risks that your potential clients are up against.

We are all in this together.

You are part of an ecosystem and your success depends on the success of the whole. Take the initiative to support those affiliates, vendors, partners and referral systems that feed oxygen to your team.

35

Beware the saviors of your cause.

When times get tight, there will be many self-proclaimed saviors. They will offer to rescue you, but these heroes don't come free. Remember the story about the wolf guarding the hen house? Watch out for their intentions.

36

Failure is a very powerful teacher.

Fail often and early, and soon you will be soaring. The toughest lessons viscerally settle in your bones never to be forgotten. No academic learning can match the raw power of wisdom learned in the fire.

Decision Making with Discernment and Guts

37

You never know what will work.

You never have enough information. It's like gambling in the dark. You follow your best hunch, go for it, see the feedback, and rework the plan. Sometimes it is entirely about the commitment you put into it.

Have plan B when A fails.

Mind-map and get the big picture of how things interlink and impact each other. Take action on plan A, get feedback, and when plan A isn't working, shift to plan B. You will also need plans C, and D, and maybe even Z.

39

Know the end game and flex.

Have your vision in clear sight and be flexible on the path to get there. It is like taking a cross-country trip knowing flat tires, blizzards, road closures, floods, traffic jams, car breakdowns, and food poisoning will shift the trajectory.

40

Seat of pants school of flying

You will be flying by the seat of your pants. Keep a wide-open viewfinder, scanning for ideas, alliances, opportunities, and partnerships that can support your vision. Be open, but not reckless, or you'll find your pants on fire.

41

Strategic and innovative thinking are vital.

Knowing the pain point is essential. What keeps your target market up at night? And don't forget edgy is good. You need to be leaning out and hanging over the cliff to anticipate where the silent hunger lies and untapped hidden potential resides.

No, you don't have two months.

Whether to take on a venture capital investor, hire for a key position, commit to a contract, make a huge equipment purchase, or move to a larger office space can be decisions that require making quick judgments without adequate information. Welcome to the start-up world.

43

Don't get bitten in the buns.

You will have misers and spendthrifts among you. If money isn't managed carefully, those with big egos will be scheduling first class airfares, luxury accommodations, and unnecessary technology upgrades before you know it. Keep your own eyes on the cash flow.

44

Road blocks and dead ends happen.

Don't waste your energy pounding the steering wheel. Breathe, back up, turn around, take stock and get creative. There is another road. Pull in your creative folks and brainstorm. You will find another path that will be even better.

45

Giving up and letting go hurts.

In this journey you will find it necessary to let go and keep letting go and it will be painful. Sometimes it will be relinquishing relationships, other times it will be ideas, strategies, pet projects, dreams, or pride. And it will be necessary, over and over.

46

Utilizing outside perspectives and trusted advisors

This is a sticky wicket. You need outside perspectives, however your advisors need to really get who you are and what you are about. In the early phase, advisory boards rather than corporate boards can be more helpful and don't have the same legal liability.

The People Part
of this Game

47

Don't promise too much early on.

People will get irate when you take something back. It is tempting in the early days to give equity to employees to reward them for the risk of joining, however if advisors and investors enter, the percentages of ownership will get diluted.

Check backgrounds on all potential hires.

Take the time to check out new people you bring in the company. It is easy to hire, but hard to fire. If you get red lights, pay attention, listen, and do further checking. Ignore warnings at your own risk.

49

Outliers and those who think differently

Hanging out with people just like you feels good, but in a start-up, you need decision makers, thinkers, problem solvers, idea folks, and relaters. You want a balance of personalities and qualities. Group-think will kill you.

No square pegs in round holes

Carefully put people in their right roles. You can't sand off the corners of square pegs. They will be unhappy, try to change their job descriptions to fit them, disrupt, and undermine your company culture.

51

Tight shoes create blisters and bunions.

If an employee isn't the right fit, say goodbye early. Like ill-fitting shoes, the longer you wait, the more painful it becomes to move. Tensions rise, relationships fray, guilt rises, and feelings of betrayal overwhelm.

Yes, there will indeed be drama.

Deadlines hit, differing agendas clash, investors squeeze, employees quit. Some days will feel like a bloody soap opera-- and you will survive. Keep you sense of humor and a box of Band-Aids handy.

53

No, this is not a family.

No matter how tempting, don't pretend the company culture is going to be like a family, or your employees will treat you like they treat their families. Ouch! Competition for favorite son and parental projections on you will be scorching.

54

Speaking of family in the business

If you have real family members in the business, get your turf lines clearly defined so you know when to call foul. It really helps if your talents are distinctly different. You don't want two quarterbacks calling plays or you'll need outside referees.

55

You want to mortgage our what?

Your family will be impacted by your involvement no matter what. What is your family's tolerance for risk? Have critical conversations with your family before involvement with a start-up about how they feel about long hours, tight finances and any mortgaging proposals.

56

A start-up is a torrid affair.

A start-up will take over your life. You will be thinking, strategizing, worrying, having nightmares, and talking about it 24/7. It means long hours, more time with colleagues than your spouse, and getting more passionate at work than at home. Can your marriage survive?

57

Stars that glitter can create glare.

It is tempting to draw in stars to a start-up, especially technology or sales stars, but you really need team players. Dealing with tense situations and finding creative solutions to big challenges requires tight and trusting solid collaborative relationships.

58

Business will outgrow the entry team.

At some point your business will grow beyond the starting players. Phase two folks need to be specialists in each critical department. This transition time can be painful because of the emotional ties that bond people in the early birth of a company.

59

Infuse new blood into the company.

Don't get too cozy. Keep new people, new information and new ideas flowing into the business. You need input from a wide range of people, industries, and cultures so your ideas don't get stale and dated.

Watch out for groups that "silo."

When you grow and need more space, it can be tempting to let groups distance from each other. They stop communicating. This can get dangerous when groups compete for resources, or make it easy for groups to get tunnel vision and myopic.

Red Tape can Strangle, but Beware

61

We can figure this out ourselves.

Or maybe not! It is very tempting to try to wing it yourself when money is tight in the beginning, but it can also be foolhardy. Get legal advice you respect and trust early on. It saves heartache and legal snafus later.

62

You need a red tape champion.

Get someone on your team who thrives on crossing the t's and dotting the i's, filing the reports, and reading up on the laws and legal procedures. Don't take it on if it isn't your cup of tea, or you'll end up gagging on it.

63

Protect this precious newborn you've conceived.

Identify what you need for protection of intellectual property; trade secrets, assignment of invention, patent, etc. Can your invention be reverse-engineered? You don't want your infant kidnapped.

64

Even though it feels so heartless

Get solid non-compete, non-disclosure, non-solicit, independent contractor and employee agreements from the beginning. These agreements define the rights of each party. It is harder to get formal agreements later when your relationships feel cozier.

65

Sometimes a tight constraint gives protection.

If you are a creative type, it can be hard to deal with all the legalese and rules that hem you in, but they also keep you safe. When up against it, you will be thankful for the straightjacket that kept you protected.

66

One omission can be totally devastating.

The devil is in the details. What happens if an early shareholder dies? Do you have key-person insurance? Are early shareholders protected when later ones come in? Can you fire an early shareholder? Consider all the possibilities you're sure won't happen.

Leadership with Wisdom, Courage, and Compassion

67

Inspiring the troops can't be faked.

You must have real passion for your cause and love to inspire others if you are leading an initial start-up company. Inspiration coupled with innovation is the magic formula that will draw in the creative talent that you need.

68

Self-Reflection--do you embrace it?

You better know your strengths, your weaknesses and your hot buttons. You are going to get pushed to your flash point more often than you'd like. Take a deep dive into your psyche before it's too late.

69

Does your EQ match your IQ?

Can you read people? Are you a good judge of character? Do you understand body language? Can you manage yourself when others are hostile? Can you handle being skewered in very tense situations? These entrepreneurial survival skills are essential.

70

Get alignment with the whole team.

In a small start-up it only takes one person to derail the system. Get the entire team on board with the vision and the strategy. Smoke out any naysayers and get them with you or out the door before they contaminate the pool.

71

Don't do what you can delegate.

If you are an owner or CEO and beyond the very early stage, don't do what you can delegate. Do what you do best and delegate the rest. You need to be leading, strategizing, and empowering others.

Group decisions eventually need to stop.

Initially everybody wants a say in every decision. That builds cohesion and union. As things start to move fast and become more complex, however, you need more efficient decision-making processes.

73

Leadership is helping others to shine.

Leadership involves mentoring and coaching others. This requires seeing the hidden talents in others and calling them forth. Rejoice in the growth of folks you mentor. They will in turn want the best for you.

Find the balance with information transparency.

This is a delicate tight rope. People need to know enough to support the mission, do their jobs well, and trust the leadership. On the other hand, salary figures, or the status of some pending negotiations are by nature confidential and should stay that way.

75

Filter out the noise that distracts.

A critical lesson is learning what and who to listen to. Key employees and advisors, good friends and valuable customers may be on your "listen-to" panel. The wrong voices can get you off track. Keep the wisdom, discard the static.

Stop nasty rumors in their tracks.

When harmful rumors are flowing in your company, nip them in the bud. Such things are cancerous and like mosquitoes they feed on blood. Call out the source and put the rumor to rest. Then look for any systemic root cause that needs to be addressed.

77

Develop balanced optimism for your sanity.

Know your strengths, seize opportunities and weigh the risks. Can you live with the worst outcome? Can you mitigate the risks? Everything you do is an opportunity to learn and even if something doesn't work, it often leads to something that does.

78

Leverage all your resources and ideas.

Look at all your connections and their connections. Examine how what you are doing could be amplified by partnering with someone else. Look for unusual ways to apply your product or service in a totally different arena.

Get the inside scoop on partners.

Know the mindset of outside partners and customers whom you need to get launched. If they are frozen in fear or old institutional patterns, will that block you from getting launched? Who and what are essential for your launch?

Remember the "Tar Baby" children's fable?

If you go from clarity to fear, you can get stuck in tar. You won't be able to discern friend versus foe. You risk being backed into a corner, and losing control of your vision and your company. Fear is not your friend.

Managing Yourself is a Fulltime Job.

81

Activate your self-start button now.

It is all up to you—no boss breathing down your neck. This is the exciting part and the scary part. Now is your chance to show your stuff. You have been talking this up for a long time. Let yourself shine!

82

Self-discipline--your relationship with time.

Time to get organized and clear about priorities; don't get lost in Facebook. Take time each morning to get focused. Your ability to use time well has never been so critical. Harness time or it will harness you.

83

Embrace blurry eyes and groggy mornings.

You are going to work 12-hour days and 6-day weeks for a while. Caffeine will be your friend and your enemy. Watch out for the roller coaster of sugar and caffeine highs and lows. Think carefully about choosing foods that will fuel your brain.

If you are micromanaging, question yourself.

Micromanaging is managing, not building a company. You have just bought yourself a job. Look at your own fears that are getting in the way. It is time to learn about letting go. You need qualified people and they need to soar.

85

Perfectionism is death to a startup.

One of the biggest challenges for many start-up individuals is releasing impossible standards. To get something launched, given all the obstacles and challenges, will require some throttling of your sacred cows.

86

Upgrade your emotional cruise-control skills.

Learn some tools to cool the fire when your buttons are pushed--deep breathing, yoga, tai chi, meditation, running, whatever works for you. Use them daily, don't wait until you need them, it's too late then.

87

All your underwear is gonna show.

Whatever your hidden drivers are--ego, greed, power, money, control, etc.--they will be seen in the light of day by those around you. Take stock and get honest with yourself about your psychological shadow.

88

Freezing, flight, or fight won't do.

Learn some good conflict resolution tools that will teach you how to really listen, build rapport and find common ground. Get comfortable facing conflict--no hiding under the table, threatening, or avoiding phone calls.

89

Monsters under the bed at night

Potential contract signing that keeps getting dragged out, promised investment that never comes through, partner betrayal, vague promises, technology that never seems to deliver what it should, bills that are overdue, delayed payroll. All these and more will be popping up in your dreams.

90

Deeper in, the tighter the screws

The more in debt, the more you become beholden and tempted to sacrifice your values. Do you bail, file bankruptcy, damage your credit and reputation, or hold on and trust there is a light at the end of the tunnel?

91

It helps to admit your mistakes.

You will screw up many times so get used to acknowledging your errors. There is much to learn and many faux pas to be made. Eating humble pie will ease you through a lot of tough situations and endear your colleagues to you.

92

Tim Westergren pitched three hundred times!

Take a lesson from Tim in resilience. He persevered through three hundred pitches before getting investment to keep Pandora alive. Don't give up after the first or tenth no. Say, "thank-you" and keep going.

Ending or New Beginning, you Choose

93

When to step back, let go

There will come a time when the company is up and running and you will itch to go start something new, see that the growing company needs a different person in your role, or be tired and need a break. That's O.K.

When the flame has burned out

New innovations make you obsolete. You can't maintain market share. The culture has moved on—think Kodak and telephone landlines. Sometimes you just have to shut down because that is the only thing to do.

95

What an amazing ride it was!

When you do step off the roller coaster it is a loss, much like a death. You have the experience that you were in an alternate universe. You don't know what to do with yourself—time feels weird. Where have you been?

96

Business degree plus several years' analysis

Your experience was an amazing education combined with a full disclosure of your psyche. The experience has changed you and you won't be quite the same ever again. What you have learned about business and about yourself is invaluable.

97

Up for air--detox and recovery

Catch your breath, take a break, get out in nature, reflect on what you have learned, and give yourself time to do all the things you missed. Play, get together with friends, take a hike, take a trip—just cruise for a while.

98

Stages of grieving-- denial, anger, bargaining

It will seem strange to go through the grieving process, but it will happen anyway. You wander feeling lost, reflect on mistakes, feel angry about the betrayals, are glad it is over, and miss it all at the same time.

99

New beginnings-- accept, feel, adjust, reinvest

With time comes healing. You accept what was, the intensity fades, you forgive and let go. You begin to explore what might come next. You start to get curious about how to use that hard earned wisdom.

100

Shall we do it again? Huh?

Did I really say that? How can I possibly want to go through that kind of intensity again? But it is so exciting, and the sky is the limit, and we can build something that will really make a difference. Why not?

See the entire Six-Word Lesson Series at *6wordlessons.com*

Learn more about starting a successful business at coachforlifechange.com